Around the Table

Gathering People Together and Building Relationships

Christy Ogden

Copyright © 2022 by Christy Ogden

All rights reserved.

No portion of this book may be reproduced in any form without written permission from the publisher or author, except as permitted by U.S. copyright law.

Contents

Endorsements		V
1.	Chapter 1	1
2.	Chapter 2	4
3.	Chapter 3	6
4.	Chapter 4	8
5.	Chapter 5	10
6.	Chapter 6	12
7.	Chapter 7	15
8.	Chapter 8	20
9.	Chapter 9	25
10.	Chapter 10	31
11.	Chapter 11	35
12.	Chapter 12	41
13.	Chapter 13	44
14.	Chapter 14	46
15.	Chapter 15	48

16.	Chapter 16	52
17.	Chapter 17	54
18.	Chapter 18	56
19.	Chapter 19	58
20.	Chapter 20	62
Chapter		67
Acknowledgements		69

Endorsements

"We have known Christy most of her life, and she has been an impact player since junior high. *Around the Table* is a great read to help face life's uncertainties with confidence. Much has happened around the Sudan and Ogden tables. We are fortunate she has invited us to sit and reflect with her. May God powerfully use *Around the Table* to impact you."

—Dr. Byron and Carla Weathersbee, Co-Founders/Executive Directors, Legacy Family Ministries

"I have had the joy of knowing Jordan and Christy for many decades and their respective families. There is so much I can relate to about the "table." Having 7 children of our own and 14 grandchildren I am drawn back to the successive tables we have had over our family journey. Christy does a remarkable job of connecting table fellowship with seasons of family life, deep rootedness in community, generosity in life and intentional suggestions of how to develop your own rhythms at all stages of life from raising young children to empty nesting. A wonderful, practical and spiritual read."

—The Rt. Rev. Philip H. Jones, Lead Bishop, Anglican Mission in America (AMIA)

"The breakfast table and the dinner table were central to raising our kids to love God, love one another, and grow in community with family and friends. The table done well changes the world. We could not be prouder of Jordan and Christy Ogden and their family and are so excited about this fresh practical look at how to make the table a place of renewal, connection, restoration, and communion with God and each other. Read it, enjoy it, apply it, and let it change your life and the family and friends that gather around your table."

—Jimmy and Laura Seibert – founders and leaders of the Antioch movement.

"As a mom of 6 children and grandmother of 2, I highly prioritize time around the table. Some of our fondest memories have been made there. The table is where we gather for so much more than meals – laughing, crying, connections, worship, life

– finding strength in God and each other. It's worth fighting for. The stability the table provides families is so powerful.

Through the years at our table, from extended family, friends, missionaries, exchange students and more, we have grown and benefitted. There is no greater blessing and joy to me than to have many ages and life stages around my table. Christy's book beautifully highlights the critical importance and rewarding aspects of this practice."

—Pam Jones

Chapter 1

Thoughts on the Table

(from my dad)

The table was obviously where we ate meals, but it was also the place where we had conversations. Whereas a lot of families would retire from the table to the living room to talk, we would often stay at the table to carry on the conversations. Luana (my wife), was not a great cook, but she was a gracious hostess and was always willing to have an extra person at the table. And in that way, family felt bigger than just our immediate household. The table was also the place where we had family devotions. We did not do it on a consistent basis, but when we did, it was at the table. The table was where Luana and I would talk after the kids had gone to bed or were doing homework. It was where we'd make decisions for our family. It is the exact same table that has been in the exact same spot for 37 years. The table is where we would play board games, much as we do now with the grandkids. Now, there is a TV beside it, but there was never one when the kids were growing up.

My dad participated, but it was my mom who was the impetus behind these times. Unfortunately, those times are over as my mother, who has been living with Alzheimer's Disease for over a decade, is no longer around, but in a memory care center. Below is a post about her that I wrote in 2019 for my dad's blog: **alzheimershubbydoc.wordpress.com**

When I think about my mom's Alzheimer's, it is hard to think of how it has impacted me in just one way. It has been such a long road as I have worked through her diagnosis emotionally, and it affected me in different ways in each season. I remember that she first started having visible symptoms during my youngest sister's wedding. We were eating lunch at a restaurant, and we realized my mom couldn't write a check to pay for the food. It broke my heart. At the same time, I realized I was going to have to take up a new role. This new role would not only include experiencing the loss of my mother, but also, as the oldest sister, taking on the role of looking after my sisters in a maternal way to make sure they were doing okay.

Another snapshot I have is around 2012 when we were thinking about moving to Michigan. I remember asking my mom and dad what they thought, realizing how much things would change with me being far away (my family lives in Texas), and not being able to help as much as I would want. I remember my mom and dad so clearly telling me that they wouldn't want her diagnosis to stop me and my husband from responding to God's leadership in our lives. Making that decision to move has definitely changed my experience with mom and her Alzheimer's, because what I experience with her now is more in snapshots rather than seeing the slow, steady decline that other family members see. It has also caused me to grieve a little more quickly because of not being able to see her as often or talk to her on the phone (since she could not really use it very well).

The loss has felt so great, and what I hate the most is that my kids haven't gotten an accurate representation of who my mom really is. When we first moved to Michigan, she would still come up and stay with us for a week at a time and was always amazing with the kids and was so present with them – which was so helpful due to my challenges as a young mom; I love that at least my older kids got that from her. As her disease progressed, she wasn't able to come visit by herself anymore and eventually she couldn't come up at all.

I have another clear memory from a couple of years ago on the first day of school. My fourth was starting kindergarten and my youngest was in preschool. I remember that night after all of the excitement and stress the day held, making sure everything was ready for all 5 kids to get off to school and the prep work that had happened. My husband was gone for work and I was at home feeding the kids dinner by myself. I suddenly had this overwhelming grief. I realized there was no one to check on me that eventful day. I wanted my mom to say, "Hey, how did your kids' first day of school go and all the stress and all that that held?" In that moment I became aware of another way I'd feel the loss; only a mother knows what that feeling and experience is like and can really look after a daughter in the way that you need at that time.

I recognize now that while there is so much loss, and I hate that I don't have my mom here to ask me those questions or care for me and to let me ask her my questions, she is actually closer than I realize. I had this realization a year ago that there's a lot more of my mom inside of me than I had previously recognized. I know I have her laid back yet intentional style of parenting, and her way of always creating a hospitable environment for people who come into her home. And although I don't have her to ask specific questions, I now understand that she had been training me my whole life to do this.

In closing, this is what I have realized: As you do the hard work of rearing your kids, you equip your kids to do life without you, since you will not always be there. And while I would much rather have her mentally and physically with me, I am thankful that my mom gave me everything she did in the days when she could. It shaped me to be the mom and person I am today, and it is shaping those around me.

Much of Mom's equipping and shaping of me happened around our table. That is what this book is all about. I wanted to start with that blog entry so you can feel the mingling of loss and gratitude that I have for my heritage, in hope that we will all seize the precious moments we have together around our tables.

Chapter 2

The First Table

It's funny that I decided to write a book titled "The Table" at this time in my life. Two days before I started writing this, a *huge* table was delivered to my house. This wasn't any ordinary table. I had been telling my husband, Jordan, for years that I thought we needed a bigger table for our house. We had the space for it, and as our five kids were getting bigger, we just didn't have a lot of extra room for the people we welcomed into our home on a weekly basis to sit. But before I talk about this table, I want to describe each of the tables we have had since we have been married.

The first table we ever had was an antique table from Jordan's great-grandmother, Gan-Gan. It was a beautiful table that worked well for our 600 square foot apartment. The first time we sat people down at our table was the day we came home from our honeymoon. Jordan told me, "We are hosting our community group here tonight!" We literally had to take the stickers off the new plates and utensils from our wedding gifts that day. We served a simple meal of baked potatoes that night, but had great conversations around that table. We were creating community as young adults, in a city we were all getting used to, and in a stage of life that was new to us all, having recently graduated from college. What did this new life look like and how were we going to make it without the comfort and security of college life and its schedules? We slowly figured it out and had many, many meals around that small table; we never let the size of our table or the smallness of our apartment stop us from welcoming people.

I eventually decided that we needed to refinish the table as it was so old, and I wanted to see what a new finish would look like. So, Jordan enlisted one of our good friends to help us restore this beautiful piece of antique furniture into what it should be. The crazy thing about this friend is that he had a vision for families eating around tables as well. Little did he know that one day he would quit his corporate job, and risk it all to start building tables and make a place for people to gather. It's so fun to watch your friends at the beginning of their calling, and see it develop. I love that the famous Clint Harp was a part of our first table. Working under our Knox Street apartment carport in Dallas, Clint restored that old table to its original beauty.

Chapter 3

The Second Table

After a couple of years of eating at the beautiful antiqued table, we realized that we needed something a little less "precious" and a little bigger for all the people we were having around our table. We lived on a street where I could walk to Pottery Barn, so I could go there often and see what items were on sale, and keep my eye on anything that might be marked down. One day, I noticed this beautiful mahogany table was for sale as a floor sample, and discovered that it had a leaf available to make it even longer. I came home and told Jordan all about my discovery. Amazingly, he was very supportive and so we made our very first big-ticket purchase as a young married couple. I was so happy and so proud of the "big kid" purchase we made, and of course wanted to buy chairs to go with the table. That is when I learned how incredibly expensive dining room chairs were. So, we decided to keep the antique chairs that went with his great-grandmother's table. We loved that table and hosted hundreds of people around it.

Later, that table went with us as we moved into our first house. The best way we knew how to love people was by bringing them around the table, serving them food and hearing their stories. I learned with that table just how to make a great table setting where matching placemats, napkins and plates can make a statement and elevate a regular dinner to something special. But, I also realized that paper plates and napkins can serve a similar function when something special is not needed. It was all about giving people a sense of home and safety. Some days called for nice china and others called for paper. And almost every day called for fresh flowers in the center, because those are always important! We had that table as the centerpiece of our home for the entire time we lived in that precious Austin-stone house on Concho Street in the middle of Dallas. We brought our babies home to this table, and they sat with their chubby legs around it once they graduated from the high chair. The table was extended with a leaf every time we hosted Easter or other holidays with all of our family, and anyone else who didn't have a place or family with whom to celebrate. It was a great table.

Chapter 4

The Third Table

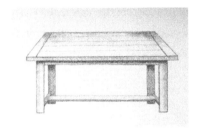

Our next table was built when we were moving to Michigan. At that time, there were many tears shed at the table, but also excitement about the new people who might be brought into our home to sit around the table. Before we put our house on the market, our realtor brother-in-law told us that we needed to take down the pergola in front of our house for better curbside appeal. We did what he told us, but had some heartache taking it down. This was a place where our baby swing hung, and we spent many, many hours sitting on the stone bench under the pergola watching our kids and the neighbor's kids playing soccer, baseball, or whatever was the game of choice in the front yard; under the pergola was where our family life really began.

One of our friends, Donny Tapie, took the wood from the pergola and decided to make it into a table. He was going to sell it, but then, before we moved, he decided to give the table to us as a gift; this is how we got our third table. It was a table that reminded us of our past, but also gave hope for our future. It was a 'stone of remembrance' for us.

One of the first memories I have from around that table was shortly after our team had moved to Michigan. We all ate one-pot pasta together around the table, wondering what our future might hold. We were eager and excited, but terrified all at the same time. However, we knew that we had the table where we could come together to encourage, strengthen, strategize, and build each other up. And that is exactly what we did. We brought our church planting team together around that table, we loved them, cared for them and told them that they had what it took to start something from scratch in this region.

Then, we started meeting people in the city and inviting them into our house to sit around our table. tableWe were so surprised by how many people that we had invited to our table, had never been invited into someone's home for a meal. After we heard that many times over, we realized that inviting people to our table should be a core part of our community-building strategy. It was something that just came naturally to us as we had been doing it our whole married life. Thus, we started inviting the new people that we met to that new table, and they came and sat around the table with us. The table that contained our past and our future, became a place where our new friends shared their own past and dreams of their own future. Some people came once and we never saw them again, but others came and kept returning. We had one family that came and the mother became one of my closest friends. At the time, she was a single mom with two daughters who needed a place to share the pain of her past and be given hope for her future. As she kept coming and sitting around our table, the Lord began to do amazing things in her life. He brought freedom to her life, emotional and spiritual health and even a new husband along with two other kids. As I mentioned earlier, at this time (early 2020) I was feeling that we needed a bigger table. We had moved into a new house and my kids were getting bigger and we needed more space so that we would be able to host more people.

Chapter 5

The Fourth Table

Jordan knew how I felt, so he asked my dad to build me a table for Christmas. My dad was excited to build a table, because he loves building things and was wanting to use redwood to do it. Jordan's family owned a lumberyard (Sligh Lumber Company) and there was a lot of left- over lumber that had been sitting there for 50 years. There was a lot of redwood that was in amazingly good condition. Normally redwood is used for decks and outdoor projects, but he wanted to try it for an indoor table. Here we encountered a similar theme: the past mixed with the future. The old wood with a history of the Sligh Lumber Company (Jordan's mom's side of the family) was given new life in the form of this new table.

So now we have a huge nine foot long by four foot wide table sitting in our dining room. It has history, as well as beauty and love, that has already been etched into it before we have even started having people sit around it for a meal. I can't wait to see all that God does around this new table; it's going to be fun.

Chapter 6

Why Tables are Important to Me

This past fall, I had a revelation about the importance of tables in the midst of our family grappling with my mom's declining health. As mentioned earlier, my mom was diagnosed with Early Onset Alzheimer's Disease (EOAD) over a decade ago, in 2008. It was devastating news to receive as you can imagine. I was a young mother with a one-year-old and another child on the way. I couldn't imagine what it would be like to slowly lose my own mother, or how I would be able to learn to be a good mother without her input and encouragement. Thankfully, she was still functional enough to be able to love and encourage me for approximately the first five years of my learning motherhood. In addition, she was still able to play with my kids and love them even beyond that time. But slowly, as this ugly disease does, it took her away from us. It was a painful and slow loss, but real nonetheless. Each time she would come to visit, she could do less and less. I was able to see it more clearly than my sisters, because I only saw her several times a year and the differences were more striking. I could even see it as I looked back at pictures and could see the subtle changes of the loss of life in her eyes.

That summer of 2019, our family decided that it was time to move mom into a memory care facility, something that none of us ever saw ourselves doing, and didn't want to do. Seeing the wear and tear that caring for my mom had taken on my dad up close, coupled with the state of my mom, I realized that it was time to do something different. I told my dad that we had already lost mom, and we couldn't afford to lose him as well. He had 16 grandchildren that needed him, and we needed to make a change. After discussion and figuring out what was best, we decided on a wonderful place for my mom. The date was set and we made plans accordingly. I wanted to be a part of the move (I am the oldest sibling of four, so you know I like to take charge and be a part of everything, as your typical first born does). So, I flew down to Texas and together, the four siblings drove the hour and half drive from Dallas to Waco, not knowing what was before us. My sisters and I wanted to make sure my mom's room was super cute, a place that reflected her personality, and that was inviting for us to come and visit her, as well as a place in which she would feel comfortable. So, after a quick lunch with my dad at our favorite local sandwich shop, we headed out to shop with dad's credit card in hand. We spent the entire afternoon shopping for all of the necessities (and non-essentials) for her room and were so happy with our purchases.

After shopping, we headed back to the house for one last dinner together as a family of six, and with my mom still living at the house. We knew it was going to be emotional, but didn't quite know how emotional it would be. As we gathered together, I was struck by the importance of the table that we were all sitting around. It was then that I realized that this love for having people around the table wasn't something that started with my generation. I had simply walked out in something with which I had grown up, having watched my own mother. I started thanking God for all of the people that my mom had hosted around the table: the lonely, the scared, the hungry teenager, the college student missing his family, the new family in town, my basketball teams, my college sorority friends, extended family, friends that felt like family, and every one in between. There was a sacredness about the table and all that happened there. It was at that special moment as we had our last dinner together around that table as a family, when I realized that the legacy of gathering people around the table was not going to stop with mom moving into a memory care facility. Because she had multiplied her life in so many ways, all of her children, as well as her grandchildren, continue the legacy of having people at their table.

My brother, Jason once wrote in my dad's blog what it meant to him to gather around our family's table as we were growing up.

When I think of home, I think of our table. The table at 5600 Woodcastle was central to our household. It connected to the kitchen, so whether you were cooking or eating, everyone was together. It was as if there was a magnet that drew you to the table.

That's where we spent late nights talking.
Family dinners, morning breakfasts with the newspaper spread throughout the table.
Midnight chips and salsa with my sisters.

It was a part of our everyday life. It seemed as if several times a week someone, not in our immediate family, joined us for a meal.

In my family now, our goal is to gather at the table for dinner every night. We are training our kids in how to ask questions and how to have good manners. It's a circus or a zoo, but we know it's worth the effort. We also invite people into our home for dinner regularly. It's where our kids do art and create. It's becoming a centerpiece for our family as well.

Chapter 7

Growing Up Around the Table

While around the table at that last supper together, I also reflected on what it actually looked like to be at my family table growing up. Unlike my family, which has had four different tables in our twenty years of marriage, my parents still have the same table they have had the whole time they have lived there – 37 years. My dad still remembers getting that table. They were in The Woodlands visiting some of their best friends. While the husbands were playing tennis and other sports, the moms went shopping in Spring, Texas. My mom found this table and came back to ask my dad whether they could buy it. He then went with her and bought it and loaded it up on top of their station wagon and drove it all the way back to Waco. I remembered that we prioritized eating together as a family. My dad was a doctor and that was before the day of hospitalists (doctors who take care of patients in the hospital, but who do not see outpatients), which meant that he saw patients in the office and then after work, went to see patients in the hospital as well. Therefore, most nights were unpredictable as to when he would be home for us to eat, but we always waited for him. It didn't bother my mom that the casserole might be cold or that the milk poured into our glasses was warm; we waited so that we could be together and she prioritized that.

Hearing my dad's reflection (see earlier), and from growing up in their house, I realized that if you want to host people at your table, you have to cultivate the value for it in your own life first. If you don't have the value of eating together as a family, and don't make time for it, then when someone else comes to the table, they aren't going to feel the connection and meaning very deeply. The older I get, the more I realize that it is the consistency of doing the simple, non-flashy things that make way for the most impactful things. It is the decisions you make when no one sees you, that sets you up for the times that people do. If you don't have those values from which to draw upon, and which are developed in those daily private decisions, there won't be much depth to the public impact of your life.

Our table was never perfect. My mom was not a great cook - she had a sign in her kitchen that said **"I kiss better than I cook"** and it was perfect. I'm sure that only my dad could confirm whether the sign was true or not, but I am going to assume that it was. Her lack of cooking skills, however, didn't stop her from hosting people at the table. She didn't have to have a clean house or a perfectly curated tablescape to invite people in. Sometimes it was burned rice and sometimes it was a delicious meal, but we realized that it was never about the food or the tablescape. I feel like with our Pinterest and Instagram world, we have this desire to curate our lives in order to make the perfect table setting or food before we invite people to join us. Don't get me wrong, I enjoy a good tablescape and a well-cooked meal, and I do try to do that most of the time when hosting people. But I don't want the absence of those things to be an excuse not to have people come to sit at my table. I want to have an open hand with my house and my food and my life, so that people can drop by any time and they feel welcome to have a seat at my table.

Their table illustrated that there was a partnership between my mom and dad. My mom set the stage which helped bring people in, but my dad was there too. Together they were offering wisdom, insight, asking questions and loving on people. They did whatever was necessary, and they did it together. Neither thought more importantly of their place or seat at the table, and they realized that they needed each other to make it work. I fully realize that this is not everyone's experience. Many of our friends did not grow up with both parents in the home, or if they did, both parents were not always working together in partnership. If this was not your experience, but you still desire to have a special table experience in your home, I want to encourage you to go for it, and start a new chapter in your family's heritage around the table.

A lot of training happened at the table. Earlier, I mentioned the warm milk that sat on the table. Do you know how many times I had to sit at the table after everyone was finished, and drink the warm milk because my parents were training me? They trained us through the topics we talked about, the conversations we had about our day, or school or world events. There was natural training for life and relationships that happened every day around that table. Perhaps it was the amount of time and energy invested around that very table that made the last meal together such a sacred moment.

After realizing the sacredness of the moment at the table, the six of us then ate our last meal together. It was beautiful and sad and all of the different emotions that are felt when you are walking through something like a season ending event. We then walked into the living room next to the kitchen and decided to have a time of prayer. I wanted our last time in the house as a family to be spent in the presence of God. It was beautiful. We worshiped God through tears and praise. We prayed for healing yet again, but also stated that we trusted Him in whatever the result. I am reminded of the young Hebrew boys in the book of Daniel and their response to the Babylonian king when he was about to throw them into the fire. *"If we are thrown into this blazing furnace, the God we serve is able to save us from it, and He will rescue us from your hand, O king. But even if He does not, we want you to know, O king, that we will not serve your gods or worship your image"(Daniel 3:17-18).* And that is when I realized:

This is where one's roots in God are both activated and developed.

- Your roots in God are developed in the midst of pain, hardship, suffering, the darkest days of your life.

- They are developed when you are in a place that you couldn't even imagine ten years ago, and you realize that this is where you *activate* the places of your faith.

- This is where you draw upon who God is and what God can do.

It is also where your roots in God are *grown*. My roots are able to go deeper when I am able to continue to praise God and worship Him even in this dark place. This is where they go a bit deeper and are able to hold me up even more.

Earlier this year, my six-year-old nephew was diagnosed with leukemia (Acute Lymphocytic Leukemia), and the first thing he said when my sister and brother - in - law told him that he had cancer was "that's ok - cancer will get defeated because God always wins!" Wow - what a response! But that response was only able to be activated because it was already developed inside him in the first place. That's why we do countless training sessions with our kids. That's why we teach them the Biblical truth of who God is and who God says we are. You never know when they are going to need it. If those truths weren't there, then from what would this six-year-old boy have to draw when he was faced with a big enemy like cancer? It's the same for us. This is one reason we do the spiritual disciplines. It is why we spend time in God's Word, and we memorize Scripture and we learn to pray. It is because no one knows when the cancer diagnosis is going to come, when Alzheimer's moves to a later stage, the affair is revealed, the betrayal happens or the job is lost. When we have the truth of God in us, we can activate it when we need it. That was what was happening to us that night. We were *activating* what we already knew about God, but it was also going deeper and deeper into the core of who we were as a family, so that when the next thing happened (like our nephew's diagnosis), we were able to draw on what was already there. In addition, these events that happen shape our faith. Our faith does not grow unless it is tested by times of suffering. Each time we experience one of these episodes of suffering and we see God respond with His grace and power, it is like a stone of remembrance or a well from which we can draw the next time we face a new challenge.

The question we all need to ask ourselves in relation to this is *"what are you building into and what will you have to draw on when you need it?"* Legalism won't be enough at that time. Just going through the motions of church and religion won't get you through either. The time you spend depositing God's truth and character deep within your soul is what is needed for you to draw from. We also need to make sure that our children have something to draw from as well. Will they know who God is and be able to let that truth navigate the murky waters of things we don't understand? It matters. All the little things that we do for our own spiritual development and for your kids, if you have them, matter. Bring them to the table - whatever that might look like - and show them the way.

Chapter 8

Seasons at the Table

I never really thought much about seasons until I moved to Michigan where there are four distinct seasons. I grew up in Texas which consists of two seasons: hot and cool. You really don't get the cold, crisp air of fall and the smell of fire pits and changing of leaves until about the middle of December. I have come to love the seasons so much more, once I let myself enjoy them for what they are. I live in the Midwest now and here we have beautiful fall colors. The leaves changing colors and every Pinterest quote about fall really comes to life! It's almost glowing when you get the peak of the color change of the leaves - I love it! After a couple of autumns up here, I found myself almost dreading the joy of the leaves changing, because I knew what came after the leaves changed color - they would then fall off the trees and the trees would be bare for the next 5-6 months. I was self-protecting and not allowing myself to enjoy the beauty, because I didn't want the winter and all of the misery that brings, to come. But, after a couple of years, I was able to recognize what was happening in my heart, and I decided that wasn't the way I wanted to live. *If you dread what comes in the next season, then you miss out on the season right before you.* I had to learn to enjoy every brilliant tree that I saw and capture the blue sunny days that made the leaves glow even brighter, because even though it meant a new season was coming, I would hate to miss the joy of the one before me.

I recognized that I can do that in life as well. I can miss the beauty of what is going on before me, because I am fearful of a hard season ahead. I am a futuristic person by nature, so I am constantly looking towards the next thing and the next hill to climb. Thus, at times I miss all the beauty around me, and the lessons and the things that God wants to teach me in the present. Once I learned to appreciate the seasons, I was able to embrace them all, even winter. The winter season lasts way too long here in Michigan. There is no rosy way around that fact. If winter lasted just the 3 months allotted for it in our seasonal calendar, I think I would like it a lot more, but we can have a huge dump of snow here around Easter and even into May. It can be very depressing, and I try to channel my inner spring by wearing brightly colored clothes and earrings, pretending that it looks like that outside. The other hard thing about winter for me is that I don't see any signs of life. You can only go for so long without seeing life, until it affects you more than it should. But there is also a lot you can learn in the winter, if you just take the time and energy to look.

The winter has a slowing down effect that happens naturally with the short days and the cold temperatures. It beckons you to eat a bowl of hot soup around the table and read (or listen to) a book around the fireplace. You don't want to go outside and you can't do as much anyway. There is beauty in this season because it brings us all a little closer and centered into our family life. The fall is busy with the start of school, sports and holidays that create a lot of hustle and bustle, but winter brings us all in. A snow day blankets the entire world in white and calls for baking competitions between my kids, hot chocolate and popcorn after playing in the snow, as well as a good board game or movie. There is something comforting about the slowness into which this season forces us. It gives us time to rest and store up energy for the next season.

If it wasn't for the barrenness of winter, we wouldn't be able to see beyond what is right in front of us. When there is no growth on the trees, you can see beyond. Isn't that a gift at times? Don't we need to have that barrenness to know what is actually going on in our lives and in those around us? It gives us space to see the terrain and to make adjustments. We don't get distracted by the fullness of life because everything seems bleak and despairing. As I walked and realized this, I was stirred to allow God to show me what was the terrain of my heart and what is really going on inside me? I prayed, "Use this season to show me what you want to call me into, and how you want to lead me in this next season". This is all good stuff, but what does it have to do with a table?

I realized that there are seasons around the table as well. There are seasons when we sit around eating dinner together every night. During these times, we can go slower and deeper into our conversations and what we are going after. Then, there are seasons where life is faster paced, and where we might only get two meals together because our nights are filled with baseball practice, soccer games and youth groups. This is where you have to make a choice. Am I going to capitalize on the time we have together at the table? Am I going to use these two meals to bring community and connection and training to the table? Or, am I going to let my idealistic ideas that I am not eating dinner around the table together enough, derail me from the times I do have?

I have seen this time and time again when working with people: We let our perfectionistic ideals rob us from making progress in the long run, even if the short term is not what we would like. No one does anything perfectly all of the time. No one. But we think that because we aren't making the mark on our goal of spending time with God, or eating together around the table or working out, then we should just give up altogether. This is robbing us of actually living the life we want to live, because we let perfectionism take the lead. We have to get up and keep trying even when we don't achieve our standard. In some seasons of life, eating around the table two times a week is okay, if that is all the time you have, and if you actually make it meaningful. I will caution you that you shouldn't accept this as the norm for your life. Regular family dinners are associated with lower rates of depression, and anxiety, and substance abuse, and eating disorders, and tobacco use, and early teenage pregnancy, and higher rates of resilience and higher self esteem (). We do have overloaded lives and that makes for limited time around the table. It is robbing us and our kids of really important investments into one another's lives. So please, don't hear me say that you shouldn't arrange your life around making this a priority. However, there are seasons in which you can't gather around the table as often as you would like, and that is okay. You have to give yourself grace.

It isn't a season if you do it all the time. So, recognize the difference between the two. If you are in one of those seasons where you don't have more than two or three meals around the table a week, then capitalize on those times you do have and make the most of them. There are seasons when you have a bunch of little kids at home. This season won't last forever, and what happens around the table then, is very different than when you have all school aged children. Then, it is even more different when your kids are in high school. Your table time might be five-minute dinners at the most, and that's all right. You are training them and you won't be in this season for long.

When our kids were little, we started using this time around the table to train them how to have conversations with one another. We recognized that they were all talking over each other and *it was so loud*! I heard about a question game on a podcast, so we borrowed the idea and have been doing it for the past ten years. This was one of the best ways we were able to bring sanity to that season around our table. We would start by having one child ask someone else at the table any question they wanted. The next person would answer the question, and then the one who asked originally would have to ask a follow up question based on the answer that was provided. We would go around the table until every person had a chance to be the one asking and the one who answered. We loved it, and still do, because it trained our kids to be good question askers. But it didn't stop with asking the question. It trained them to listen to the answer so that they could ask the follow up question. It also trained the listener to actually listen to the question so he could give an appropriate response. In addition, we had them look the other person in the eye, whether asking the question or answering one. It caused the table to be quiet and centered, and it gave everyone a chance to talk, which is important in a big family with a lot of loud people. We still do the question game, but not every night.

Our children are older now, so we have more discussions about current topics, and they like to ask a table question. For those unfamiliar with the term, a table question is simply a question we put out there for each person to respond, in an attempt to get everyone into the conversation. It may be something simple like "What was the high and the low point of your day?" Or it could be more thought provoking like "What famous person in the past would you most like to meet?" We still incorporate what we learned from previous seasons, but we recognize that kids change and their needs change with different seasons.

The seasons are shifting here in Michigan. It's a little brighter than normal and it is making my heart so happy. Maybe this year will bring the gift of a shorter winter. I noticed the birds coming to my porch and I saw a few buds, the first signs of life. I think I'll embrace it, because who knows when a long winter will come again. There could still be patches of winter that come back this year, but I am training myself to live each day in the present and what God has before me, and not look too far ahead or behind. I am learning to lean into whatever season He has given me and be thankful for it, and trees have helped me understand this.

Chapter 9

Trees, Roots and Fruit

Tables can be made of many different materials, but all of my tables have been made out of wood. There is just something special about wood. I think the major thing is that it comes from trees, living things. The Bible has a lot to say about trees and its uses can be good or bad. The cedars of Lebanon were used to build Solomon's temple. In Isaiah, we see that they were used to build a fire but also to build an idol. And lastly, we see that a tree was used as a cross to hang the Lord Jesus.

I've always loved trees. I love the big trunks and the leaves and the shade that they provide on a hot summer day. I love the glory that comes when trees change colors in the fall, and I love the beauty of the new green that appears on a tree when spring finally comes around. One of my favorite chapters in the Bible is Psalm 1:

> *"Blessed is the one who does not walk in step with the wicked*
> *or stand in the way that sinners take*
> *or sit in the company of mockers,*
> *but whose delight is in the law of the Lord,*
> *and who meditates on the Law day and night.*

> *That person is like a tree planted by streams of water,*
> *which yield its fruit in season and whose leaf does not wither -*
> *whatever they do prospers."*

I love that the tree mentioned in this passage is a tree that makes it for the long haul. It yields fruit in season and its leaves do not wither - because it is connected to the source of life - the water. I have thought long and hard about being the oak tree that does not wither. I want to be strong, bearing fruit into old age. How does this happen? I want my life to be a tree that provides shade to those who come into its presence. I want to be strong and steady so that it is a safe place for others to come and rest beneath it.

I also want my life to bear fruit. If I'm honest, I actually want my life to bear lots of fruit, because Jesus said, "My Father is glorified when you bear much fruit" (my paraphrase of John 15.8). I want my life to do just that. When we moved to Michigan in 2013, it did not appear that our lives were bearing lots of fruit, nor any fruit for that matter. We didn't know anyone in the city to which we moved, and we were there to plant a church from scratch. It was slow growth. I saw other churches (in our movement) that started around the time we did, and they had lots of fruit quickly, and it made me jealous. I wanted what I saw in those other churches, and I wanted it now.

God quickly showed me the importance of the root system that we were building underground. He showed me this through studying His Word, and by reading a great book by Banning Liebscher called "Rooted". Most recently, God has shown me this through what I am labeling my personal theme song titled, "I will Rise" by Kristene DiMarco. The lyrics state, "underground is where life begins, my heart will rejoice in the hiddenness". The season of the underground is way more important than I had ever realized. While the fruit above the surface is great, what God really wanted to do in my life was to build a root system underground that could handle the giant oak tree that I wanted my life to represent.

God started showing me that faithfulness in the little things, and the season of hiddenness, has great value in building something that will last. I have always been taught to prioritize the primacy of seeking God first thing in the morning. But it was at this time that God showed me that this was also a big part of building my root system. I had to have constant nourishment and water for my soul, if anything that was built above ground was going to last. This is similar to the Psalm 1 passage in that the tree was planted by streams of flowing water. It came in the time spent in those quiet, secret places, where the nourishment of this root system was taking place., I wasn't to concern myself with what I saw 'above the ground,' but to be faithful sowing into the places that no one sees.

It struck me as to how different this was from the world system in which we now live. With Instagram and all other social media platforms, people can immediately see the "fruit" of someone's work and that person can become an overnight "success". It's awesome in some ways, because it removes obstacles and what used to seem impossible by putting your face out there for anyone to see, and getting immediate fame for it. But it reminded me of the growth that you see in the weeds around you. They will shoot up and you think "wow, I have some life here" but then you can pull it up quickly and it is gone! There is no rootedness or weightiness sustaining it. This growth looks good above ground, but it has nothing there to uphold it when the hard winds and storms of life come. Winds are actually good for a tree in that the movement that occurs when it is young stimulates the root system to grow deeper and stronger, so when the strong winds do come, it will be able to withstand them. To be an oak tree that is flourishing into old age, I have to develop a root system in the underground and unseen parts of my life that actually gets stronger when winds and hardships come.

When I think of storms, I don't have a lot of experiences in my own life, at least in the early years. I grew up in a very healthy family that wasn't perfect (whose family is?), but was safe and secure and I had few hard things happen to me. I would say that the first "storm" of my life came when we were trying to get pregnant. Jordan and I got married right after graduation from college. We were high school sweethearts, and although we went to different colleges, we stayed together and after graduation, were ready to get married and start our life together. After a couple of years of marriage, we were ready to start our family. I have always wanted to be a mom, and I had my timeline as to when I wanted it to happen. I wanted to be 25 just like my mom was when she had me. Everything up until that time had gone according to my timeline. There hadn't been many bumps in the road, and my planner self really liked that.

I am sure you know where this is headed. Getting pregnant did not come as easy to me as I would have liked. It was a hard season of trying, having friends all around me get pregnant and start families and me not getting pregnant. It was even more painful to have patients that I cared for in the hospital, who were so young and had gotten pregnant accidentally, while I was not able to do something that seemed so natural. After a while, we started down the infertility track and it was a very emotional time. I learned about disappointment with God and was learning how to cope when life doesn't go your way. We were also learning how to lead a church at this time, and that felt like a storm in itself. We were 25 years old and became pastors of a church where most of the people in our congregation were our peers, and many were even older than us! It was a hard transition for everyone, and I had trouble seeing which way was up.

When these storms were raging around us, I learned the importance of sinking my roots deep into God's word and prayer. I couldn't control things the way I like to do, but I could control my response and my decision to continue to seek God and His face, and learn from Him in this time. I learned then about taking my disappointment to God, and how to deal with pain and suffering. I learned how to get wisdom for situations and decisions we had to make on a leadership level. I learned that I had the choice as to what to do with the pain. Would I choose bitterness or truth? The roots were going deeper and deeper. I was becoming stronger and less shaken by the circumstances and events. The roots were going down decision by decision. It was at this time that I started learning about my emotions, and it really was a rollercoaster each month. I'd rise up hoping, praying, doing treatments for infertility, and then fall down the other side with disappointment, fear and sorrow. It also taught Jordan and me how to come together as a couple amidst things that we didn't understand.

After months and months of trying to get pregnant and trying different fertility options, my doctor came to me with something she had found during her examination. She said that she found endometriosis in my uterus and that could be the cause of the problem. She said that she had an opening that week for an ablation that would clean out the uterus, and it should make it to where the next month I could try to get pregnant. Maybe this was the answer we were looking for. If you have ever tried to get pregnant or know someone who has, you know that each month is important and you don't want to waste any time. I came home from that appointment and told Jordan that we could schedule the surgery in two days, but I really wanted us to seek God to determine if this was the right path for us. It was very strange in that we had always felt such a release from the Lord to go forward with fertility treatments, and we would usually just get a sense to go with it. For some reason, this time I felt the Lord saying to wait and really ask Him if this was where He was leading us.

Jordan came back to me and said he really sensed that God was initiating with us to do what he described as a "10-day push". This would consist of 10 days where we would go to the different lifegroups in our community and have them pray and worship over my womb and ask God to heal it. We asked that the places where endometriosis had caused scarring to occur, not allowing life to form, would be cleaned out and made new. We also happened to be in the middle of a time of prayer and fasting for our church. Remember, we had just started leading, and Jordan called us to 40 days of prayer and fasting as a church. (Good way to make everyone love you as a new leader). I sensed that what God wanted to do in me in the natural, He would do in the spiritual for our little church body. He wanted to allow the scarring from past pains and hurts in the different people be healed, so that new life could come forth in our church.

It was challenging, but I immediately connected with what Jordan suggested. He was inviting us to do this faith challenge with our community amidst the pain. Deeper and deeper, stronger and stronger, the roots were being developed. And so that is what we did. We went to different friends and families' houses for ten days straight and had people pray and worship over my womb. It was a holy and special time, and it really was another part of allowing God to make my roots go deeper into Him in the midst of the pain. Well - as you might have guessed - we got pregnant in the midst of the "10-day push". Now, let's be clear.

I am in no way suggesting that this is a fail-proof method to get pregnant. It is not even a "method" at all. It was simply what we felt that God wanted us to do. I have walked alongside many friends who have tried to get pregnant for years and years and have been unsuccessful. I don't pretend to understand the ways of God. I am merely relating my journey in a time of suffering.

That challenging time solidified the truth and reality of who God was for us. Did we believe that He was good in the midst of not seeing the answer to the things we were asking for? I recognize that our season with infertility was not that long compared to a lot of people and people that we very deeply love, who are still walking this pain out. But that doesn't take away from what God was doing in us through this process. I realized early on that I can't compare my pain and stress and challenges to other people's. What may seem like a bump in the road to some, may be a place of deep pain and heartache to others. By nature, we compare our circumstances with others and it either makes us feel better or worse about our own situation. But what God has taught me through the years, is that it doesn't matter how things compare on another person's "scale" of pain and challenge. What matters is my heart's response to it. What matters is how I find God in the midst of it. I find Him in the dark, secret places of my soul that no one else sees and knows. I need to find strength, comfort and care from God in those places, so that when the next wind or struggle comes, I have something that will support and sustain me in it. Little did I know when we were walking through that season of infertility, that it was only the beginning of a long season of pain, specifically related to my mom's disease and the long slow path of suffering that would follow that. I love the way God used our infertility story to bolster our faith as we watched Him show up and help us by giving us the grace we needed at the time. It was one of those stones of remembrance that gave us the confidence and strength to face the trials ahead. He is so creative and is not formulaic in how He chooses to work. What He wants is not for us to have a new baby or to even experience a miracle, but to develop a relationship with us. I think that is the whole point of the table. It is a place that allows relationships to happen. It brings people together and slows us all down.

Chapter 10

How To Manage the Rhythms of Life

I have been thinking a lot about how some seasons around the table are pretty slow and others are extremely fast. Each offers its own struggles and its own opportunities.

A few years ago, the nation (and world) was struck with a global pandemic which we all knew as COVID-19. At the time, we were living in Michigan, and that was one state that was very aggressive about shutting things down. We were all in this place of "social isolation" which was so weird and hard for everyone, especially an extrovert like me. We couldn't go to a restaurant to eat, meet in groups of more than 10 people, have an in person church service or even our lifegroup at our house. We were allowed only to shop for what was necessary (or online), and had to be away from people (six feet - remember social distancing?). The gift I now see in this time is that it forced us to slow down. I am naturally a fast person. I like to go at life full speed ahead, and don't know how to stop and smell the roses. I like to accomplish things, work hard, run hard and get things done. But back then, I was being forced to slow down (besides the fact that I was having to learn how to homeschool my five children and keep all the wheels turning to run a household of seven). I couldn't run to a bunch of meetings (hello video meetings) or do a lot of unnecessary errands, or even drive my kids to school and their sporting activities.

So, what did I do with the slow? Was I going to learn the message of the table and the way that Jesus lived his life? He teaches us the beauty of slowing down and lingering. I stayed a few more minutes to let Barron tell me every detail of his story. I asked the guest(s) at my table another question so as to hear his heart a little bit more, and make a place for him to feel known and loved. I wanted to come out of COVID-19 with a new perspective on life. I wanted to be realigned to the things that really do matter and how to live daily with a clearer view of life. Maybe my running around isn't all bad, but what part of it is too much? I can only really find out when I slow down enough to allow God to speak to me. Sometimes, God forces these times on us and He certainly did this time in a big way. Then, I can only find the grace to walk that out when my roots have gone down deep into the truth of who God is, and that He can sustain and nourish me during these times.

But now, I find myself in a very fast or busy season with one high schooler, two middle schoolers, and two upper elementary kids. I realize how thankful I am for the slow seasons that we had. The older I get, the more I realize the benefit of laying the foundation of dinner around the table when my kids were younger and I had more control over our schedule.

Busyness does not have to diminish the centrality of gathering and relationship around the table. Admittedly, busyness is not the ideal, but when evening activities increase for a season, that is the time to be even more intentional as you plan for your table times. My husband and I take time to think through the weeks and months and try to anticipate which evenings will have reduced time for gathering and relationships. Because we recognize that certain evenings will not permit robust relational conversations, we seek to maximize the times that we do have on those busy evenings, and be especially stalwart on the other evenings so that the family maintains connection with one another. Each family's desire for and tolerance of activity level will differ, but the planning element can apply to all.

As you read a book about having people around the table, you might find yourself in a situation similar to ours. We are a busy family of seven with five kids spaced six- and one-half years apart. Our nights are often filled with practices, games and homework and everything in between. My husband and I realized that even in the midst of this busy season, we needed to be intentional about bringing each other around the table.

There are a few things we have done to help during this season of life. First of all, we limit the number of activities our kids do outside of school. We try to limit them to one extracurricular activity per season. Sometimes we flex on our rules and that's fine, but for the most part we limit what they do to just one. We also try to strategically put them in activities that might line up on similar nights to lessen the number of nights out. We recognize that we can't always control this, and as they are in school sports as well, we are at the mercy of their schedules. But when they were little, we would put two of them on the same team even when they were not the same age. Another thing we have done that has helped during these busy seasons, is that we have had a family meeting where we discuss the week ahead. Usually, we do this on Sunday night over dinner. We talk about what each day will hold and our kids really enjoy knowing how to prepare for the week ahead. We might have several nights of games, so we plan and talk about which days they really need to prioritize homework, and which nights they can have more play time. Jordan and I also look at which nights would work best to have dinner around the table. It might mean that we do an early dinner because the games are later, or vice versa, but it at least gives us a brief connection with all of us together with food around the table.

Another thing I have found in these busy times, is that what we have sown in the early years is starting to pay off now in the latter years. We might not have as many times around the table, but we have had the training and the practice of living around the table, so that when we do come together, we can easily engage in one another's lives intentionally because of the hard work done in the earlier years. I've thought about that with our '*Pancakes and Proverbs*' that we do on Saturday mornings. Those were very spiritually forming for our kids. And while we might not get to do that every Saturday morning these days, topics that we poured into them during that season are able to be built upon during our dinner times now.

The main encouragement I have during a busy season of life is to be intentional about creating times that you do gather around the table. I have found in this time of our lives, if I am not intentional with planning my meals and thinking about the week ahead, we could be eating cereal at 9pm every night - *scattered and not gathered*.

You might make a goal for what a win is for your family during this time as to how many times per week you gather around the table. It will be different for each family, but this is something you and your spouse should discuss. This also might be a season where you utilize some of the other things we have talked about, when you are at the table and not at your home, at restaurants, etc., to be intentional as well.

No one is perfect and no family has awesome nights every time they eat around the table. You have to give yourself a lot of grace. And along the way, enjoy it all!

Chapter 11

Holidays at the Table

I love holidays! I have always loved celebrating and have loved to do simple things to make people feel celebrated. We have hosted many holidays around our table, and one of my favorite things is making the tablescape feel special and in season for whatever the holiday is. I think about things I want my kids to remember when they grow up - the smell of pumpkin bread in the fall and fresh greens and whites that they see when they walk into the house each spring. I always have made it a point to do special things around the table.

One of my favorite things that we started doing when the kids were in elementary school was to make a special Valentine's Day dinner for them. Instead of Jordan and me going out to celebrate our love (and trying to find a babysitter who could watch them on that day), we decided to celebrate our love *with* them. I make a fancy dinner of steak and potatoes and some other things that wouldn't necessarily be our usual cuisine. We have them dress up and we use name cards and our nice dishes. We go around and tell each other what we love about the other person. It has become a tradition and everyone loves it. I recognized when I started doing this, that it really was such a simple way to build traditions and something meaningful into the everyday lives of our family. Again, I think so many times we overthink things like this, and think about how we need to have just the right dishes or experience, but kids are so easy. Just do something a little out of the ordinary and do it year after year and they will remember it, and it becomes a marker in their lives. Just start doing it and don't worry about having it be perfect. That has become my motto and it has really helped me build some beautiful traditions in our family.

We also have birthday traditions around the table. When my kids wake up on their birthday, I have presents and balloons and banners all over the table with the special breakfast cake that we make for every birthday. The kids love waking up to it. But the thing that also makes it special, is the encouragement we do around the table for the birthday boy or girl. We each tell that person what we love about them (similar to Valentine's Day but only one person gets it this time!) I love this tradition as it really makes them feel loved and celebrated and again, it is so easy.

I started to incorporate this tradition with my friends as well. When we go out for a friend's birthday, we take time to encourage them and say what we love about the friend. When we moved to Michigan and planted the church here, we didn't have a lot of other people we knew except for our launch team, and the first few people that started coming to our church. So, birthdays were very special. I didn't realize when we were doing these encouragements, that we were building a culture around how we celebrate and love people. Several people who were from the area and new to our church, said that when they received the birthday encouragement, they had never experienced anything quite like it. It was a simple way to build people up, and it took very little time or energy, just speaking out loud what you already think about the other person. It changed lives. And it was done best when it was done around the table. Now these people who have been impacted by the simple act of encouragement (on their birthday or at any other time), are incorporating it into their own family and friend's lives. It is spreading. Don't make what happens around the table complicated, and don't think that the little steps of doing something as simple as encouraging someone on their birthday can't make a big difference. I have found that doing these simple things over the long haul really makes the biggest difference. We often overcomplicate things. Just speak words of encouragement to those around you and watch them light up with love and be impacted. In addition, it is Biblical. There are multiple verses that tell us to encourage one another. My friends now look forward to this tradition and are all sad if we don't get to do it!

Another of my favorite holidays is Easter. As a pastor's family, we were always in town and at our own table for Easter. We would have our Easter service at church, and then host any family and friends that were around for a late lunch or early dinner around the table. We usually had a honey baked ham that my mother-in-law would pick up, spinach salad, sister Schubert rolls, Billie's potatoes and anything else that was brought to our table. It was always a fun time of being together and usually a nice time to relax after a busy church weekend.

I will never forget the last Easter we had in Dallas before moving to Michigan. It was the last big holiday with our extended families before the unknown was about to happen. We enjoyed the normal food, and the kids played outside with confetti eggs turning their beautiful Easter attire into a splattering of confetti colors. My sister was the first to start crying, and then most of the adults followed after her. Things were changing and we didn't know what the future was going to hold. What would time around the table look like when we lived in a different part of the country and couldn't make the drive down for a holiday? None of us knew and that was scary. There was a lot of loss that we were anticipating, and a lot of different emotions related to the upcoming changes – some good and some bad.

It was at that time that I realized when you sow happy, life-giving times around the table, you make space for the hard times to be shared at the table as well. So many people have had a hard time in their life, but no one to share it with, or a safe place where they can just cry and let out their emotions. This has been something I have been working on personally, to grow in letting myself be vulnerable with others and to be accepting when things aren't as we would like them to be.

The table is for the good and the bad. It is for training, and it is for doing puzzles. It's for big groups of people, or just you and a friend drinking coffee on a rainy day. We want to look at the table as being a safe place for people to come with every joy and every heartache. In a sense, it is a recalibration to help you deal with all that life brings your way. The challenge is to bring yourself and others to the table on a regular basis, because you never know when you will need to process the hard news or celebrate the big win or test score. It's a safe space that allows life to happen and brings you back together.

The Easter that I referred to earlier was a really hard one, and I didn't know how I would go forward from there. But we continued to take one step at a time and found God faithful to us. We were able to celebrate many holidays with our family after we moved, and it wasn't as bad as I thought it was going to be.

I do remember the first Easter in Michigan being one of the hardest times I had experienced up here. I had five kids six years old and under, and had just experienced my first real winter. Our first winter here happened to be 2013/2014, the polar vortex winter. It was also the year that "Frozen" came out. That seemed so appropriate - Elsa and her endless winter. It was a lot to navigate. I had to learn how to drive in the snow, and how to handle having 5 kids at home inside the house most of the day. My oldest was in kindergarten but it was only for half a day, and the 2nd and 3rd kids had alternating days of preschool that would end at noon as well. So, I had to get out in the snow and learn how to manage life in it, but then I was stuck the rest of the day with all of the little kids inside. It was rough. I was also leading a team of people who were from Texas and they were learning how to manage their first winter as well. So, I was responsible for pastoring them through these new changes, and learning to connect and build relationships with the people that were starting to come to our church. It was a lot to have on my plate at one time.

I can't remember when Easter fell that year - if it was in March or April - but what I do remember is that all my friends and family who lived in the south were posting pictures of beautiful spring flowers, colors, bluebonnets, tulips and sandals and their cute easter outfits. What I saw from my front window was still death and a lot of it. Nothing had changed colors yet, and the temp had barely gotten above 30 degrees. The ground was frozen solid and there were still patches of snow in some places. I hit a really low point. I remembered back to Easters past which I experienced with my friends and family around our table and the sweet times we had. Until that point, I hadn't let myself acknowledge the hard season that I had just come through. I finally just let my guard down and admitted that this was hard.

But God spoke very clearly to me during that time. I remember sitting on my white couch with my big picture window to the right of me with bare branches on the trees and dead grass outside. The song from Amanda Cook, "You Make me Brave," had just recently come out and it was playing on my phone. I realized that it is God who makes me brave. I didn't want to have to be brave at that moment, but He was giving me strength when "wave after wave comes crashing in". After weeping to this song, I felt God reveal His empowering grace to me through John 1:16 where it says, "From the fullness of His grace we have all received one blessing after another." From Jesus, out of the fullness of who He is, we receive grace upon grace. This is a different meaning of grace than the grace by which we are saved, "For by grace you have been saved through faith (Ephesians 2:8)." The grace He was showing me was the empowering grace to do what He has called me to do. It doesn't mean that it will be easy or without pain and heartache, but He will give me His grace to walk out what He has called me to do. I am EMPOWERED by the fullness of HIS GRACE. It was a watershed moment for me. He met me in my pain and showed me that He will give me what I need to walk through what He has called me to. I am to be empowered by Him to walk in all that He has for me.

That revelation from God has changed my life. Once I realized that He will empower me to do what He has called me to do, I am able to walk in confidence in the hard things of life. It also makes me want to be very cautious and attentive to listen to what God is actually calling me to do. If He is leading me into it, He will make a way for it. When I go my own way or do something because I think it is a good idea, it doesn't necessarily have the same empowering grace behind it.

For Mother's Day that same year, my sweet sister-in-law got me a print that had that verse from John 1:16 written on it. It has been a constant reminder for me to trust God with what He is calling me to, and know that from His fullness (and not my own power) I have what I need to do the hard work. When I got to the Easter table that year, there was still pain and a little heartache as

I remembered what Easter used to be like. And there was a painful reminder when I looked outside and saw that it was still 30 degrees, when I wanted to wear a cute dress but my legs were literally freezing! But then, instead of crying and feeling sorry for myself, I knew that God was empowering me to do what He had called me to do. So, I did what I always do. I brought people over to my table to share a meal together, eat honey baked ham and all the rest. I forced myself to remember that even if it didn't look the same as it did the year before, there were new people to bring together and new memories to be made around this table. I wasn't going to lose the chance to do it again.

Chapter 12

When You Can't Have People Around the Table

There are many reasons why you may not be able to have someone physically sit at your table - distance, illness, transportation or even a pandemic. Your child may be in college and not able to make it. As I mentioned earlier, I wrote a lot of this book during an unprecedented time in our nation and the world - the COVID-19 pandemic. What that meant for us is that we could not go anywhere or meet other people if there were more than ten. That made it difficult since there are seven in my family alone.

This was an unusual time in our country, and it shook many people to the core. I can see that the Lord worked in this by bringing families together like never before. There was the opportunity, if you chose, to eat breakfast, lunch and dinner together around the table, and to even linger a while afterwards. There wasn't a lot you had to hurry to go do, because a lot of people were stuck at home. We saw families come together for walks outside (it was one of the only things you could do outside your home). There is so much beauty that can happen in these times of so much pain and hurt. I believe God wants to reestablish the primacy of the family and show us how to slow down in this fast paced "go go go" life that we live (and our family is chief among sinners in this regard).

But there is also a lot of pain that is associated with these times. Not everyone has a big family like we do, or is never at a loss for people with whom to sit around the table. A lot of people have pain and loneliness and fear about what the future might hold. Our table is normally filled not only by our own family, but others who have stopped by at just the right time, or have been invited over. (I always try to make extra food because I never know who is going to be around that needs a seat at our table. I don't want the reason to not invite them to be because I don't have enough food).

I have been wrestling with this issue of how to make space for people around the table when you can't physically be at the table together. What I have found is that in these times, where there is so much loneliness and fear, people need to know that you care, you are there for them and you remember them. Even though in many ways we had a lot going on in our own lives, with learning how to homeschool our kids and having no escape during the day, we still need to be those who look out and love those around us. Who needs to feel like they have a seat at our table even if they can't physically be there? It means I send a simple text, an audio-visual text or set up a video conference to connect with those who are in my life, and who need to feel known and seen. In times of crisis, our normal way of dealing with it is to look out for our own good and our own needs and not worry about others. But, as the church, we need to look to those around us and not be so inwardly focused. Let's be those who bring others to the table virtually, and care for them in similar ways that we would if they were in a seat across from us with a plate of delicious food in front of them. I have found the best way to get outside of the pain and heartache of your own circumstances, is to look out at other people and what they need. When I can look outside of what I am feeling, and serve and care for people, it expands my heart and my viewpoint.

Don't let the fact that you can't have people physically around the table be an excuse for not caring about the people that need to be there. And, when you are stuck inside with more time with the people in your family that you can have around your table, ***capitalize*** on it. Linger with longer dinners and conversations. Let there be more times of training and laughter. Don't let the situation steal from what God is wanting to do in and through you during these days. The table is a gift and in whatever season you find yourself, make the most of it.

Chapter 13

Five Loaves and Two Fish

What do you do when you want to have people to your table but don't feel like you have enough? I know that this is a real issue for a lot of people. Jordan and I have been pastors for most of our married life, with a big family to feed, so we know the importance of a grocery budget and wanting to be wise with our money. I will say that this has been the most fun thing about the table. It seems like there is always enough when we share what we have and don't worry about hoarding some for later. I have seen God provide over and over in times when we thought we didn't have anything to share, but felt like He was asking us to have someone over and offer a seat for them at the table. It's an invitation to not think solely about yourself, but how to give to the person in front of you.

When we first moved to Michigan to plant the church, there was a lot of hosting people at the table. We were also on 100% financial support. At times it was a stretch to host a lifegroup (our weekly small group) and to serve a meal to lots of adults and even more kids. Sure, we always had a meal sign-up sheet, but who do you think ended up with the main dish most of the time? It was during that time that God did something in my heart. I wanted to be one who didn't make decisions about what we would say yes to, or who we would have over, out of fear of not having enough. I wanted to be one that gave, not based on what I had, but based on the God who provides. So many times, when hosting a group, I would be shocked to see how five pounds of ground beef could feed so many people, or how a pot of soup kept filling bowls when I thought that surely there couldn't be any more.

Jordan and I were called to generosity, and while that generally has to do with our finances and giving money, I realized that one of our greatest places of being generous is to serve people around our table. I don't worry about what I can save for us as a family later, but I give generously with what I have. I also shifted the way I serve people. I wanted to serve out of a place of abundance. I don't want them to think that there is just enough for one serving for them, but I want people to leave my house with a full tummy and full heart. I don't want them to feel that serving in this way is a stretch for me (even if it is), but I want people to feel that they are invited into a seat at our table and that they are wanted. When I host parties, I want there to be plenty of food so people feel free to partake in whatever will make them feel loved and celebrated. It is an issue of the heart and recognizing that God is our provider. When God calls me to live generously, I don't worry about myself or having enough later - I trust Him to write the check - even if it means that I have to cut back on some other things later in the month.

The issue with the fish and the loaves comes up in other areas as well (this story can be found in the Bible in Matthew 14:13-21). When I was a young mom with a lot of needy children (remember, I had 5 children aged 6 and under), and pastoring people in church, it felt like there was no way I could meet everyone's needs. The demands on me seemed too much and I didn't know how I could do it. I remember a time God very clearly told me to give Him "my fish and loaves." God encouraged me that if I would give to Him what I had, He would multiply it for the needs around me. I didn't need to worry about having enough to give, but I just needed to give what I had. And yes, He was faithful to His word. I was able to trust Him with giving what I had, and He multiplied it, using my fish and loaves to meet the needs around me. It also gave me space to trust God and not worry about things I couldn't control. I was able to do what God was leading me to do, and not worry about the pressures I put on myself from outside sources.

Chapter 14

Hope Around the Table

I have always been a positive person. In fact, in my Strengths Finder inventory, positivity is my number one strength, so it shouldn't be surprising that I see life from a glass "half full" perspective. I can usually find the good in most situations, and I don't struggle much with depression or thoughts that take me down that path. But through years of pastoring people, I have come to realize that not all people see the world the same way that I do. We have had many people sit at our table who are in hopeless situations. People whose marriages were in a very hard place, whose children who were very strong willed and not changing, many who were stuck in pornography, or those who had a loved one with a terminal diagnosis and not seeing the healing for which they were asking. And then I had my own mom who was dealing with early onset Alzheimer's disease. We had prayed and prayed for her healing and had not seen anything near that. She was getting worse and worse, and it was taking more and more of a toll on my dad. I decided that if the gospel was true, and that Jesus was good and the one who brought us all second chances, then there must be more to hope than just 'positivity' or looking at life through the lens of a glass 'half full.' I decided to study what hope really was, so that when people gathered around our table and were in hopeless situations, I had something substantial to offer them.

The Bible talks a lot about hope, and I started to notice it more and more in the passages I read. What I realized is that when we talk about hope, it isn't about what is happening in the present. Hope comes when we have an eternal perspective as to what this life actually means. When I understand that my life is important and that God does care about it – and that it doesn't end when I am buried in the ground - I have a hope for a new heaven and a new earth where all things are made new. I can pray and ask God for Mom's healing and a change on this side of heaven. I do believe that He hears us, and that He can heal and move and act. But I also have hope that there is life after death, and I know that if God doesn't heal her before she dies, then we will one day be reunited, and my mom will be made like new with a sound mind.

Hope comes when our perspective is in the right place. So now, when people come to my table and it seems like they are in a hopeless situation, I know to give them the hope of Jesus. Because of what He has done, we are able to believe and trust Him for making all things new. I will never stop giving people hope, because that is what we all need. We need to know that there is a God who sees and knows our pain. We need to know that there is a place for change in our lives. We can trust that He can do above and beyond what we ask or imagine. Don't just hope (in a secular sense – i.e. wishful thinking) for things to get better. Give people Jesus who is the real hope for us all.

Chapter 15

The Empty Nest Table

As someone who is not in the stage of being an empty nester, I don't personally know what this is like, and I'm sure it varies from person to person. Now that we have moved closer to family and have had more opportunities to relate to both of our parents who are empty nesters, we realize that it is important for us to be intentional about inviting over those who might be in the empty nest stage. Normally, I would have thought to invite over a young single adult who doesn't have any family at home, but after living with my dad, I realize it's valuable as well for him and my in-laws to be invited over. My encouragement is to look around to see who in your circle might be in that stage of life and who you might invite to your table. As a younger family, when we would invite an empty nester or an older adult into our home, I would encourage my kids to have thought beforehand about some questions to ask them. We want to value the different generations, both above us and below us, and what better way to grow and learn than to do this sitting around the table. A good question to ask an empty nester, or a grandparent, would be something about their childhood or something that has changed from when they were a child. This is so important for us, but also for our kids to realize that the world has not always been as it is now, and to be able to learn and grow from the different challenges and experiences that others have gone through.

Living with my dad, who is an empty nester, has helped me see what he has proactively done to help build relationships around the table. Here are his thoughts on the matter:

> *As Christy's father, I have been an empty nester for the past 16 years. Most of those years were with my wife as a couple, but for the past two years or so she has been in a memory care facility, so I am now not only an empty nester but also alone. Over the years, as a physician I have had hundreds of conversations with patients who are by themselves as empty nesters or completely alone as an individual. These conversations stem around poor eating practices which are very common in these situations and which are very important to me as their doctor. It is hard to cook for two people, especially if you have been cooking for a whole family most of your life. And then, as you get older, you just get tired of cooking altogether. And if it is hard to cook for two, you can imagine how hard it is to cook for just one. The bottom line is that elderly empty nesters do not eat well. But nutrition is just one part of the story.*

> *Empty nesters also desire community. When a couple is young and by themselves, it is not a problem. They are just getting to know each other and their whole lives are ahead of them and there is plenty to talk about. But when a couple has been married for 40 – 60 years, a huge part of their lives is behind them and there is little left to discuss. Community can be met in a variety of ways and the couple, or individual, does not need to just sit back and wait for someone to call. They need to be proactive. This may involve church with home groups or Bible Study groups. It can be*

family, friends, neighbors, sporting events, plays, movies, and so much more. But the call from a younger family to join them, even if it is your child, is a highlight of the week. You have no idea how much that can mean in the lives of older couples.

But there is another side to empty nesters that I want to discuss. We do not need to be pitied. We are not worn down from taking care of kids all day. We have time and most of the time more resources to be the ones to initiate gathering. For most of our married lives, my wife also loved to gather. I'm sure that this is where Christy got her love for it. We were always having people over, and while Luana was not a great cook, nor did she have a perfectly clean house, she did not let any of these things stop her. I tend to be more introverted and so I was not really energized by having people over, but I really loved when we would have young people in our house (which we did a lot). I loved the stimulating conversations as they were young and idealistic and we would have great debates.

I really believe that were she still able to, she would still be gathering people together – her family, for sure – but also people from all walks of life. And this is my encouragement to all of us empty nesters. Be proactive. You can still be a gatherer and can still foster relational exchanges. While you may not want to invite over a whole family of six or seven (though you might), you can invite a single woman or man to dine with you. With age are wisdom and experiences, and you have so much to offer. And believe me, young people do like to hear stories of long ago (which for them might be twenty years). They generally don't want to be preached to, so be creative in how you steer the conversations, and even prepare beforehand with table questions.

But it doesn't have to be a young person. Invite over a fellow empty nester, especially a widow or widower, who are the loneliest of all. There is so much good that happens when we gather together as people – and there is no better place to gather than at the table. If you read the Bible, you see that Jesus spent an awful lot of time gathered with friends and others for dinner at a table.

Chapter 16

Taking the Table on the Road

As much as I love having people over to sit around my own table, I also enjoy eating out with my family. Yes, it may be more chaotic and more expensive, but it saves the time and energy of prep and cleanup. So, what does it look like to bring the concept of the table to when you are dining out?

In some ways you might have more capacity to establish connections with people around the table if you are intentional about it, because you are not having to do the hard work of preparation ahead of time. The idea of the table is to gather and to foster relationships with one another. What I found, especially at a restaurant where you might not be on someone's home turf, is that if you are not intentional about the time, then the loudest voice or the person who talks the most is going to take over. So, you have to walk gingerly around the subject if you're with others who are not a part of your immediate family. But I find this is a great time for a table question. You can politely ask the other people at the table if they would be open to having a table question to foster discussion over dinner. As we stated earlier, everyone desires a deep and meaningful connection with other people, but sometimes we just don't know how to make space for it. By giving yourself a few minutes beforehand to think of a couple of easy questions, starting with surface questions, and then moving the conversation to a deeper level as people start talking and getting engaged.

Another beauty of being around the table at a restaurant, is that it is a great opportunity to love on the people that are serving you rather than just treating them as an anonymous figure. We have at times asked the waiter or waitress if we can pray for them, or just engage in meaningful conversation where they feel known and seen. Sometimes they are caught off guard and they don't know what to say, but most of the time they are happy to have us pray, and they find some need for which they would like prayer. Generally, we try to pray right then with them in a quiet and unobtrusive way, but if the person is uncomfortable or the situation is not right, then we will pray for them later by ourselves. Occasionally, they will really open up and tell you what has been going on in their life, and this is a great opportunity to share the Gospel. Obviously, you need to be respectful of their work load and not take them away from their job, but bringing that same relational intentionality and connectivity to every person you come in contact with, accomplishes your goal for the table, wherever you might be.

We have tried to limit phone use at the table, even when our kids were young, to create an environment for connection. One thing that frustrates me is to be at a restaurant and see a group of four young people, all of whom have their phone out and using it. Phones can be distracting in so many ways, and phone use totally defeats the idea of connecting relationally at the table. That said, we have to set a good example by not pulling our phones out as well. A good idea is to turn it on mute. It's obviously easier, and at times we have done this as well, to give a squirmy toddler a phone to play with so they stay put during a meal. But we have tried to limit that, so we can train our kids to sit at the table and be engaged even when it's challenging. It's a great time to help younger kids hone their tic- tac-to skills on a paper napkin, so you need to be really intentional in helping them stay engaged.

Chapter 17

Bringing the Table to Others

When I started this book, I lived far away from my family and so this connection to bringing the table to someone wasn't quite as clear to me. But recently, my family moved to Texas where my husband and I both grew up. My mother, as I mentioned earlier, is in a memory care facility and has declined slowly and significantly the past fourteen years since her diagnosis. When I moved back, I didn't know what my role would be with my mother. I hadn't lived in the same city as her since college, and certainly not since she had progressed in her disease. After settling into our life in Waco, I decided that the best way to be consistent in visiting my mother, and helpful in loving and serving her, would be to feed her lunch a couple of times a week at the facility. I found this to be a practical way to serve my mother, but also something helpful for the caregivers at the facility.

One time when I was feeding her, I realized that this is what it looks like bringing the table to someone who can't go to the table themselves. There is nothing glamorous about it. In reality, it is quite painful having to feed your mother, but there still is something powerful in the practice of dining together with someone that you love. It made me think that the table isn't always about conversation and dialogue, but it can be about connection and about self-sacrifice, and about valuing people even when they can't give you anything in return.

This simple act of bringing the table to my mother has affected me in a profound way. The value of people lies not in what they can do or achieve, but simply in that they have been created in the image of God. I've also noticed that while I am feeding my mother, I am able to minister to others in the dining area with whom I might not normally have been in contact. At her facility, most of the residents are elderly ladies and while I am not able to have long or deep conversations with them, due to their dementia, I find there is great power in a smile, giving a hug, or just bringing the love of God into the place.

Over Christmas, we wanted to be able to include my mother in some way and to show value in such a way that all of the grandkids would be able to see the sanctity of life, even at the extremes of age. We originally had planned a movie night at the theater in her facility, but alas COVID changed our plans as COVID often does. So, while we weren't allowed to go into the facility this year, we decided that we could still bring the table to my mother. We found out from talking to the director that we would be able to meet outside in a courtyard in front of the facility. It was equipped with tables and chairs, and with a lot of room for the kids to move about and play, and we could bring my mom out there. Therefore, we changed plans and brought the grandkids and pizza and met outside and in doing so, we brought the table to my mother. I am not sure that she knew any difference, but the kids loved it and in the process were taught an important lesson.

I think that is part of bringing the table to people - valuing people that don't have anything to give - and showing them (and us) that we can be flexible and intentional even when life looks different, and not how any of us would like for it to be. We sang Christmas carols to my mother and another resident who came and wanted to be a part as well. It was a beautiful time of celebrating life around the table (even though it was not my table) when someone couldn't come to it by herself.

Chapter 18

Gathering at the Table Without Eating

Many people came to our table when I was growing up, but not all of them came to the table for food. As I have described above, my parents regularly had people over for meals, but we also gathered around the table for purposes outside of eating.

As we got older and began to grapple with more complex ideas, we discussed them while we were gathered around the table. When a family member or someone connected to our family needed counsel, that counsel was dispensed around the table

A lot of the memories I have around my table growing up did not revolve around food. I remember sitting at the table after a basketball game discussing the highs and lows with my parents and what I could have done better and in which ways I did well (That was mostly my father – my mother always thought I did well). I also remember my parents sitting at the table after we had gone to bed, talking through a situation they might have needed to discuss or process. I remember coming home from college and sitting at the table and talking about politics or what I was learning in class or a friendship with which I was struggling. The thing about the table is that when you have created it as a space of gathering and relationship, you don't need food to create the atmosphere. In my parent's home, the table continues to be a place where, when we are all home for the holidays, we still sit and gather.

There is something powerful about a table. My kids go to a classical school now, and I remember when I was touring the school, they showed several classrooms that had big tables in the classroom rather than individual desks. Their philosophy was that a table is a place where dialogue, debate, and discussions can happen. This is exactly what I have been trying to communicate. You're centered around something that helps bond you together, even if your views and how you see things might be completely different. The idea is that it is hard to criticize a person when you are looking him in the eye, directly across the table. You can argue with his ideas, but not the person. This is a challenge with social media. People can attack the person because they are anonymous, and there is no relationship. I love how the school has developed that and I desire to continue to cultivate that in my own home. We have had countless people sitting around our table discussing their marriages, their hopes and dreams, and just connecting about what's going on in their lives.

So, as you are creating the table as a meaningful place in your home, don't feel that it has to only be about food. Encourage your teenager to sit with you as you ask him or her about their day, work a jigsaw puzzle together or play a card game around the table during a family night. The options are limitless and require only the imagination. Find ways to bring people around the table even in the absence of food, so the table can continue to be a place in your home that fosters gathering and relationship.

Chapter 19

The Table in the Bible

—The table is not a new invention. In fact, it has been around almost as long as people have been eating. Tables were of various sizes and shapes over the centuries and reflected cultural traditions. In some civilizations, people did not sit in chairs, but reclined at the table, usually on one side resting on the elbow. Being invited to sit at one's table was considered an honor, and the places at the table held various degrees of honor.

The situation in the Bible was no different. Tables are mentioned numerous times with various meanings. The first mention of a table was in Exodus 25:23-30. Here God was giving Moses the design of the tabernacle which was a shadow of the true tabernacle in heaven. It was divided into three areas – an outer courtyard, a Holy place and an inner Holy of Holies. There were various articles of furniture and utensils in each place. In the Holy place, was a small table on which they placed the daily bread of the Presence. It was twelve loaves, each representing one of the twelve tribes of Israel. This was to show them that His Presence was with them at all times. The key for our purposes is the idea of God's Presence. If the table is to be a place where we foster the development of relationships, the key to doing that is to be present.

We see the use of tables several times in the history of the kings. Here we see that being invited to sit at the king's table to eat was a high honor. To not show up for this was a grave insult, and a liability for serious consequences. In I Samuel 20:24-27, King Saul is having a festival and David was invited, but he chose not to attend (out of fear for his life), thus arousing Saul's anger. The idea here is that the table was the central place where celebrations took place, and was where they gathered people together. While today, not showing up to eat when you have been invited is not a capital offense, it is still a major social miscue. We want to be people who honor our hosts by showing up and doing so on time. And while we do not really have true places of honor at our tables, when we are hosting and gathering, we want to place people in the middle of the action, and not by themselves on the end or amongst the kids. It would be preferable to seat them near someone they know, if that is possible.

Without question, the most popular table in the Bible is in Psalm 23. Here God prepares a table before King David in the presence of his enemies. This was a sign of deep humiliation for the defeated soldiers. And no, we do not want to invite those we do not like to our table and have them watch us eat. That is not the point. The psalm shows Jesus as our shepherd, and as the shepherd He provides for us, gives us rest, guides us and gives us victory. For our purposes, we see the table as showing God's abundant provision for us. That is why when we eat, whether by ourselves or with a group, we say grace, thanking God for His provision. It may be a little or a lot, but it is He who provides. And it is why we can still host and share with others whatever we have. We do not have to wait until the cupboard is full.

In the New Testament, we first see the table in a parable of Jesus. Here Jesus tells them that when they give a luncheon or a dinner, they should not invite their friends, relatives, or rich neighbors. For these will return the favor and that will be their reward. Instead, they should invite the poor, the crippled, the lame and the blind. In so doing they would store up treasures in heaven. It is certainly not wrong to invite your friends and family over to dinner. In fact, it is good and right. But that should not be all we do. We should purposefully invite people who are in a lower socioeconomic class or people who are not like us. It will be good for them, for us and especially for our kids.

In I Corinthians 10:21, Paul talks about eating food sacrificed to idols. We are not going to go there, but he gives the analogy between that and eating at the Lord's table. By this, he means the Lord's Supper. At that time, they ate the Lord's Supper at a table with their house church. Here we see that one of the most important ordinances in the Christian church is done at a table. We could go several different ways with this. Depending on your beliefs, you could certainly eat the Lord's Supper at your table during Lifegroup. That would be a very enriching experience. But even more so, I think for us it would mean that when we eat, we should always remember the Lord. It does not have to be dramatic. It can be as simple as saying grace and thanking God for His provision. Or it could involve a table question revolving around God's work in your life. There are many ways to incorporate the spiritual in a gathering around the table.

Then in Acts 6 we see the first quarrel in a church. It certainly was not the last. This revolved around the sharing of the food when they would come together to eat. The non-Jewish believers were being overlooked in favor of the Jewish believers. The apostles were called in to referee. Peter suggested that they get some qualified men to oversee the process so that they could concentrate on prayer and evangelism and not have to wait on tables. There is nothing wrong with waiting on tables. It is good and needed, but not an efficient use of the apostles' time and energy. The table represented the believers sharing all things and having everything in common. When we invite others to our table, we are sharing God's provision for us with others. We gather--we share—we relate. In so doing, lives are changed, and God is glorified.

Lastly, we see the table in a prominent place when we actually get to heaven. In Revelation 19:9, God invites believers to the wedding feast of the Lamb. While the word table is not expressly used, it is certainly implied. I picture a long table with chairs all along each side and the table filled with all sorts of good food and wine (or Diet Coke or coffee). I see people sitting together from all peoples, nations, tongues and tribes. Everyone is eating and talking and sharing their stories. They are laughing and having fun. It is the perfect picture of what the table is supposed to be. It is a place of gathering, hopefully of all sorts of people, sharing and building relationships. While it won't be perfect here on earth, let's give it a try. Start inviting people to your table and see what happens.

Chapter 20

Final Thoughts Around the Table

Go live the message of the table. There is so much God has for each of us as we gather and relate with one another around different tables. If there is one thing I'd like for you to take away from this book, it is this:

it doesn't have to be perfectly executed or consistent, you just need to start doing it. Start bringing people around your table and being intentional with the conversations that you have there. And trust God for what He wants to do in and through you as you build this in your life.

The longing of all of our hearts is to have meaning and connection with people, but we don't realize that it takes intentionality and sacrifice to make it happen. And as you do it, bring others along in the journey, for there are many other people who are longing for this. Look around. Who is in your sphere of life that you can invite to your table? We are about to move into a new house in the new city that we moved to, and I can't wait to bring others around the table there. I want to create new memories in a new home around the same table and with the same rhythms. If you don't know where to start, look at who is around you and ask God to show you one person to whom to reach out. Trust God, that as you start walking it out, you'll be creating a beautiful story for everyone who comes alongside you around that table. And you will make lasting memories.

I'd like to close with a blessing that I used to say over our church when we would dismiss them from our gathering time:

The Lord bless you and keep you; the Lord make His face shine on you and be gracious to you; the Lord turn His face toward you and give you peace. Num. 6:24-26

For Further Reflection

Chapters 1-5

    1. Does your table have any special historical or family significance?

    2. What can you do to make your current table something special?

Chapter 6

    1. Have there been any special times your family has gathered around your table?

    2. What are some things you can do to make the table a central gathering place for your family?

Chapter 7

1) What type of training could happen around your table? What will you do to ensure that you implement that training?

2) What are you building into (in your own relationship with God) and what will you have to draw on when you need it?

Chapter 8

    1. How could you incorporate table questions or the question game into your family's gatherings?

    2. Is there a season that you do not particularly like? Ask God to teach you something about Him or about life through that season.

Chapter 9

1) In what ways are you building a root system so that the fruit of your life will last?

2) What places of pain have been important parts of your own life? How have they shaped your view of God and how you walk it out now?

Chapter 10

1. What new perspectives have you developed during the Covid slow down?

2. Are you running too fast? What are some ways you can force yourself to slow down?

Chapter 11

1. Which holiday would be best for your family to develop new traditions regarding gathering around the table?

2. Ask God for one idea new or old to implement and then find someone in your life that will both help you and hold you to it.

Chapter 12

1. What was your reaction to the shutdown at the beginning of Covid?

2. Who is someone in your life that needs to know that people know them and care about them? How can you respond to this?

Chapter 13

1. How is God leading you to live generously?

2. Is there a place of fear that might make you think you don't have enough? What does God say to you about that?

Chapter 14

1) Where do you need hope in your life right now?

2) How does the hope of Jesus with an eternal perspective change your view of your current situation?

Chapter 15

1. Who is an empty nester that you know that you could invite over to your table?

2. What are some questions you would like to ask an empty nester?

Chapter 16

1. What thought does this chapter give you to incorporate when you are away from your own table? Maybe you can think of some table questions to have ready for the next time you go to a restaurant.

2. Next time you are out to eat, try to engage the server and ask to pray for them.

Chapter 17

1. Who could your family take the table to that is not able to come to your table? How will you make this happen?

2. What other ways can you teach your children to value those who are disabled in one way or another?

Chapter 18

1. Is there a time in the week that makes sense for you to gather others around the table to connect without food? When would it be and what would make sense for your family/group to do: talk, a game, etc.?

2. For us, the table is where we gather, but it does not have to be an actual table. Is there a place in your house where people tend to congregate? If so, encourage that to happen and make specific plans for it.

Chapter 19

1. Meditate on Psalm 23 and think about God preparing a table for you and what that might look like.

2. Think about the banquet table in Revelations 19 and how exciting that will be, and let it put hope in your life. Also think about ways you can incorporate that type of atmosphere in your home.

About the Author

Christy Ogden is a wife and the mother of five. She grew up in Waco, Texas, and went to college at Baylor University where she earned a BS in nursing. She worked as a pediatric cardiology nurse in Dallas, Texas, until she and her husband felt called to plant a church in Ann Arbor, Michigan, which they did over an eight-year period. They have since moved back to their roots in Waco. Christy spends most of her time rearing her children, but loves people and loves to host people in her home. She is also an avid runner. Currently you will find her working for a summer camp, driving her five children to their activities, cheering for them on the sidelines at their games, and gathered with her family and friends around her family's table. She is married to her high school sweetheart, Jordan Ogden.

About the Book

The book is a collection of stories and thoughts of life centered around the table. Christy draws on her own life experiences, first as a child where the table was an integral part of their family's dynamics. Then, she weaves in her own memories of life at their table with her family and hosting multiple people and events over the past twenty years. The main theme is that the table should be a place of gathering people together and fostering relationships. In it, she shares both the joys and the heartbreaks of her own life in a very candid way. But she also gives a lot of practical applications for how others can foster these kinds of interactions in their own family. The book is for anyone, but Christians will find it particularly compelling as a means to follow in obedience to God's command to love one another. If you are wanting to transform the times you and your family spend around the table, this book is for you.

Acknowledgements

I would like to thank Jordan for believing in me and making me write even when I didn't feel like I had much to say....for him always being my biggest advocate and seeing more in me than I see in myself. I'm thankful to my parents for laying the foundation of the importance of the table in my early years....for always bringing people around the table and loving them the way they are – even if it was my high school boyfriend who became my husband – eating Lucky Charms with my mom when I wasn't there. I would like to thank my in-laws for always providing a place for me at their table. I am thankful to my kids for being the reason I want to gather around the table and the fun and memories we have made through living this out. I am also thankful to them for understanding when I was off writing, and giving me encouragement. In a weird way, I am thankful to Covid in the sense that the lockdown forced me to stay at home and gave me the time to write this. I am thankful to my brother and sisters as well as their spouses for all of the times we have gathered together around my table, providing lots of material for this book. I want to thank my very talented youngest sister for the art work and book cover. Then, of course, are all of the countless people over the years who have accepted my invitation to sit at my table and share their stories. Lastly, I want to thank Annette Perez for doing the grammatical editing, and Micah Key for doing the content editing.

Made in the USA
Coppell, TX
06 December 2022